How To Use This Study Guide

This five-lesson study guide corresponds to *"How To Know the Difference Between True and False Prophets" With Rick Renner and Guest Joseph Z* (**Renner TV**). Each lesson in this study guide covers a topic that is addressed during the program series, with questions and references supplied to draw you deeper into your own private study of the Scriptures on this subject.

To derive the most benefit from this study guide, consider the following:

First, watch or listen to the program prior to working through the corresponding lesson in this guide. (Programs can also be viewed at **renner.org** by clicking on the Media/Archives links or on our Renner Ministries YouTube channel.)

Second, take the time to look up the scriptures included in each lesson. Prayerfully consider their application to your own life.

Third, use a journal or notebook to make note of your answers to each lesson's Study Questions and Practical Application challenges.

Fourth, invest specific time in prayer and in the Word of God to consult with the Holy Spirit. Write down the scriptures or insights He reveals to you.

Finally, take action! Whatever the Lord tells you to do according to His Word, do it.

For added insights on this subject, it is recommended that you obtain Joseph Z's book *Demystifying the Prophetic* and Rick Renner's book *Apostles and Prophets: Their Roles in the Past, the Present, and the Last Days*. You may also select from Rick's other available resources by placing your order at **renner.org** or by calling 1-800-742-5593.

TOPIC

False Prophets

SCRIPTURES

1. **Matthew 7:15,16** — Beware of false prophets, which come to you in sheep's clothing, but inwardly they are ravening wolves. Ye shall know them by their fruits....

2. **Galatians 3:1** — O foolish Galatians, who hath bewitched you....

3. **1 Thessalonians 5:21** — Prove all things; hold fast that which is good.

GREEK WORDS

1. "false prophets" — **ψευδοπροφήτης** (*pseudoprophetes*): a compound of **ψευδής** (*pseudes*), meaning phony, feigned, or bogus, and the word **προφήτης** (*prophetes*), which is the word for a prophet; together, it means bogus prophets, pretend prophets, or wannabe prophets

2. "wolves" — **λύκος** (*lukos*): a wolf; applied figuratively to cruel, greedy, rapacious, destructive men; the word used to describe prostitutes who sold themselves on the streets at night; hence, not God-called leaders, but those who will sell themselves for gain and only stick around as long as there is something to be gained

3. "foolish" — **ἀνόητος** (*anoetos*): brainless, non-thinking people

SYNOPSIS

The five lessons in this study titled *How To Know the Difference Between True and False Prophets* will focus on the following topics:

- False Prophets

- Angels of Light and a Counterfeit Anointing

- Judging Prophecy and Dealing With Prophetic Mistakes

- Rightsizing the Prophetic

- A Prophet's Submission to Authority

Although it may be hard to believe, the presence of false prophets was a real problem in the Church during the First Century. The Bible has a great deal to say about true and false prophets, and in this series, we will unpack how to discern the difference between the two.

The emphasis of this lesson:

Jesus compared false prophets to ravenous wolves who roam the Church, howling to get people's attention to bring them under their influence and take advantage of them. These false prophets operate under the control of a seducing spirit, drawing people to themselves instead of drawing them to Jesus.

Jesus Called False Prophets 'Wolves'

According to Scripture, Jesus was a genuine prophet. That is what He called Himself in Matthew 13:57 and what the multitudes called Him in Matthew 21:11. As an authentic prophet, Jesus warned us about false prophets, telling us:

> **Beware of false prophets, which come to you in sheep's clothing, but inwardly they are ravening wolves.**
> **— Matthew 7:15**

When Jesus called these imposters "false prophets," He used the Greek word *pseudoprophetes*. It's a compound of the word *pseudes*, which describes something that is *phony*, *feigned*, or *bogus*, and the word *prophetes*, which is the Greek word for a *prophet*. When we put the two words together to form *pseudoprophetes*, it describes *bogus prophets*, *pretend prophets*, or *wannabe prophets*.

Sometimes these individuals begin with an authentic, prophetic gift. But somewhere along the way, they get off track and become false in what they are doing. Then, as Jesus points out here, they begin operating in the Church, using a perverted version of their God-given gift for their own personal advantage.

What Jesus said next is extremely eye-opening. He said that these false prophets "…come to you in sheep's clothing, but inwardly they are ravening wolves" (Matthew 7:15). The word "wolves" here is the Greek word *lukos*, and while it is the plural term for *wolves*, there is much more to its meaning.

During Jesus' day, the word *lukos* was a slang term used to describe *prostitutes* in Roman cities. They would roam the city streets at night, howling like wolves to capture the attention of men; hence, the reason for the slang term *lukos* meaning *wolves*. The "den" of these prostitutes was the brothel where they worked. After roaming the streets at night, making their presence known by howling to attract attention to themselves, they would seduce men into their den and take advantage of them financially, reaching into their pockets and taking their money.

So when Jesus called false prophets "wolves," He was telling us that they are a category of people that roam the Church and will howl aloud to get people's attention. Speaking both sensational and spectacular words, false prophets will use any means at their disposal, including social media, to garner attention, bring people under their influence, and lure them into their "den."

Like the prostitutes in Jesus' day, false prophets seek their own advantage, using bogus prophetic utterances to seduce people and reach into their pockets to take their money. In addition to finances, false prophets are also after prestige, position, and power. Keep in mind, comparing false prophets to "wolves" was Jesus' doing, and He was a real prophet.

We Are To Evaluate Prophets and What They Say Using God's Word As Our Guide

Why does God want us to be aware of how false prophets work? It is so the Body of Christ isn't taken advantage of or abused by those with wrong motives. False prophets operate under the influence of a seducing spirit, drawing people to themselves instead of drawing them to the Lord Jesus.

It's been said that the way to tell if a stick is crooked or not is to simply put a straight stick next to it. That is how you will be able to see if something is off or bent in the wrong direction.

For us, as followers of Jesus, our "straight stick" is the Word of God. It is often called the *canon* of Scripture, which literally describes *a measuring rod*. If we will take God's Word and place it up against individuals who say they are prophets, we will see if the things they say and do are aligned with the Word of God or if they are transgressing in those areas.

With regards to recognizing prophets, Jesus said, "Ye shall know them by their fruits..." (Matthew 7:16). True, genuine prophets are going to produce godly fruit of the Spirit that is in line with Scripture. False prophets, on the other hand, will produce rotten fruit that is often carnal or fleshly and even evil in nature.

The Biggest Differences
Between True and False Prophets

Many times, in the Body of Christ, we look at events that are happening in the world and hear the voices of those who are giving their interpretation of what is going on in these end times and what may be coming our way. Among those voices, there are both true and false prophets. The truth is that in most cases, false prophets in the Church started out as real or true prophets with a genuine gift from God. But over time, something in them changed.

A true prophet becomes a false prophet when his or her *motivation* changes. It's all about motives.

If a person's motive is personal gain or advantage, and he or she is trying to prophesy other people's money into his or her own pockets, their gift has become falsified and corrupted. Therefore, it's very important that real prophets stay in close relationship with others who will help keep them in check and hold them accountable.

True prophets are easy to identify when we measure them by the Word of God. They live according to the Bible and are submitted to spiritual authority. Likewise, they are generous and have the signs of prophetic ministry working in them. Those who operate in the other fivefold ministry gifts are able to identify and acknowledge those who operate in the genuine office of the prophet.

False prophets are the opposite of a true prophet. Their character reveals that they are out doing their own thing or trying to make a name for themselves. They may look and sound biblical, but they are really ravenous wolves whose motives are selfish and self-seeking. And somewhere along the way, they know that what they are doing and saying is false. In other words, their misuse and abuse of God's Word is not an accident — *it is on purpose.*

Moreover, false prophets are unbiblical in the way they live and tend to have what we might call "out-of-Bible" experiences. The biggest motivator in a false prophet's life is often greed or the love of money, and what he does is questionable. Rather than recognize these individuals as operating in the office of a prophet, those who are genuine prophets look at them and question what they are saying and doing.

Not Everyone Who Flows in the Prophetic Is an Actual Prophet

Now, there is a segment of people who may flow in the gift of the prophetic but do not stand in the office of a fivefold ministry prophet. These individuals are what the Bible calls a *novice*, someone who is a beginner or a newcomer to the Christian faith. They may have a gift of the prophetic operating in their life according to First Corinthians 14, but because they do not really understand the gift, they operate in a gray area.

Sometimes the worst thing that can happen to a novice with a spiritual gift of prophecy is for a pastor or someone in spiritual authority to tell him he's a prophet. The pastor or leader will often see this person's prophetic abilities and tell him, "You're a prophet," and many times it's not true. Just because a person operates in the prophetic doesn't mean he is a true prophet. We need to be careful not to call people something they are not, because if we do, we are setting them up for failure.

Novices who have a gift of the prophetic in their life will eventually come to a valley of decision where they will look at the gifting they are operating in and check their heart and decide whether they *are* or *are not* a true prophet. If they will humble themselves, dig deep into God's Word, and allow the voices of genuine, fivefold ministers to speak into their life, they will be corrected and placed on the right path.

If someone decides to take the path of a false prophet, it seems that there are stages to their decline. Progressively, they move from 30- to 60- to eventually 100-fold into darkness. At 30- or even 60-fold, they may still be salvageable, but it will likely take a true, fivefold ministry person to assist in the restoration process — especially one who functions in the office of an apostle. Because apostles are called to lay foundations and bring order to situations, they are called to step into prophetic movements at times to bring order where needed.

It is during this tender time that a God-led rebuke can rescue such a person before they reach the point of no return. If they are teachable and receive the correction, they can come back into the light. In fact, just as someone can descend into darkness progressively, they can also ascend into the light progressively — from 30- to 60- to 100-fold.

Again, this decline into falsehood could be avoided if people who are gifted as prophets will keep their heart in check and remain in close relationship with others who function in the fivefold ministry gifts.

We Must Be Careful To Stay in Our God-Appointed Circle

In the book of Jude, which was written by the half-brother of Jesus, the Holy Spirit tells us about a group of people called *wandering stars* (*see* Jude 13). The Bible does not question whether these stars give light or not. They are real stars. In other words, these are people God has called, and they were emitting His light.

At some point, however, they began to "wander," which is a word in the original Greek that means they *swerved out of their God-appointed orbit*. When a person with a real gift from God begins to drift away from the godly people they've been in relationship with — especially when they stray from submission to the authority God placed them under — it is the equivalent of them moving out of their God-appointed orbit or circle.

Friend, when you move out of your God-appointed circle, there's no one to speak into your life or hold you accountable for your actions and attitudes. The people God puts in your life are like guardrails on the highway, keeping you moving forward down the road toward your destiny. Without them, you get out of balance and can be easily derailed from your divine purpose.

If you take a close look at most of the people who have moved away from truth and into falsehood, you will see that they also abandoned the rock-solid relationships in which God had placed them. And for the most part, now they are working alone. In that condition, they become deceived and begin to deceive others.

It may be that you are reading this, and you have been hurt by a false prophet. Or maybe you're someone who operated in the prophetic at one time, but for some reason you became wounded. As a result of that wounding, you swerved out of your God-appointed orbit and have become a wandering star.

The truth is, many prophetic people are a little thin-skinned, which means they can be sensitive and easily offended by others. Likewise, they can also become insecure and need to be validated — so much so that if they are not given certain things or treated in a certain way, they can begin to drift and become a wandering star. If that is what you are dealing with right now — if you have been hurt by people operating improperly in the prophetic — God wants to set things right and set you back into the proper circle of relationships He has established for you.

Please realize that anything from God can become falsified. The Bible talks about false prophets, false teachers, false apostles, false evangelists, and false pastors who are also known as hirelings. But if there is a falsified version, there is also a *genuine* version. You can't have a counterfeit without the real deal.

Filter All Teaching and Prophecy Through the Word of God

When the apostle Paul wrote his letter to the believers in Galatia, he was writing to a group of people who had been deceived, which tells us that any of us is capable of being duped by the enemy. With great concern for their well-being, Paul said:

O foolish Galatians, who hath bewitched you....
— Galatians 3:1

The word "foolish" in this verse is the Greek word *anoetos*, which describes *brainless, non-thinking people*. Paul's use of this word is the equivalent of him saying, "Oh Galatians! Why aren't you thinking? Why aren't you using your head?"

The truth is that sometimes when people hear prophetic ministry, they think they're not supposed to question it but to simply receive whatever is being said or spoken to them. However, this idea of brainlessly accepting whatever is spoken in the name of the Lord is a perfect recipe for becoming bewitched like the Galatians.

In the original text, the word "bewitched" in Galatians 3:1 means *confused*. To avoid this debilitating deception brought on by the devil, every Christian must learn to do one vital thing:

Take responsibility for what you hear and filter it through the Word of God and the approval of the Holy Spirit.

Regardless of who is speaking, we need to properly process what is put on the spiritual plate in front of us.

Be Aware of What You're Feeding On Spiritually

In the program, Rick shared about a time when he went to a restaurant in Siberia, and the aroma of the food filling the air was simply magnificent. At the same time, he noticed the unclean conditions that surrounded him on the table, the utensils, the floor — he could tell it was not a clean place and he had some concerns. But because the food smelled so good and he was hungry, he went ahead and ate. Well, not long after, he contracted hepatitis.

The lesson here is quite clear. If you're in a church or meeting where ministry is taking place, and things just don't feel right in your heart, that's the Holy Spirit trying to speak to you and direct you to use caution. Although there may be things that appeal to your natural senses, if something about the environment or what is being said or ministered feels "dirty," get up and get out of there. You don't want to contract spiritual hepatitis from sitting at the wrong table and eating from a contaminated source.

Listen to the Holy Spirit! Don't be like the Galatians, whom Paul said were brainless, non-thinking people, and who became bewitched or confused. God wants you to use your mind and test the prophecies you are hearing. That is what He tells us to do in First Thessalonians 5:21, which says, "Prove all things; hold fast that which is good."

Once you have proven and tested what you have heard and you know that it's right according to the Word of God and it bears witness with your spirit, hold tightly to what's been spoken to you that is of God, and discard everything that is not of Him.

In our next lesson, we are going to talk about angels of light and see what a counterfeit anointing is.

STUDY QUESTIONS

Study to shew thyself approved unto God, a workman that
needeth not to be ashamed, rightly dividing the word of truth.
— 2 Timothy 2:15

1. Those who operate in the gift of the prophetic need the voices of genuine, *fivefold ministers* to speak into their life to help them remain true to Scripture and on the right path. According to Ephesians 4:11 and 12, what are the five ministry gifts in the Church? Where did they come from and what is their purpose?

2. On the program, Rick points out that false prophets in the Church are often individuals that started out as real prophets with a genuine gift from God, but over time, their motives changed. How important are your motives in the eyes of God? Consider Romans 12:3; First Corinthians 16:14; and Philippians 2:1-4,14,15. What is the Holy Spirit showing you in these passages?

PRACTICAL APPLICATION

But be ye doers of the word, and not hearers only,
deceiving your own selves.
— James 1:22

1. When you realize that Jesus compared false prophets to prostitutes that roamed the city streets to capture the attention of men and seduce them into their den, how does it change the way you view false prophets? Is there anyone you've been watching and listening to that falls into this description? If so, what changes do you need to make to free yourself from falling further into his or her deception?

2. Just as it's very important for real prophets to stay in close relationships with others who can help keep them in check and hold them accountable, the same holds true for you. Who are you in relationship with right now that helps hold you accountable for your attitudes and actions?

3. Briefly describe at least one situation in which a friend helped keep you from making a foolish or serious mistake. What did that person do or say to cause you to adjust your response? Who have you helped influence in this way?

TOPIC

Angels of Light and a Counterfeit Anointing

SCRIPTURES

1. **2 Corinthians 11:13** — For such are false apostles, deceitful workers, transforming themselves into the apostles of Christ.
2. **Galatians 3:1** — O foolish Galatians, who hath bewitched you, that ye should not obey the truth....
3. **2 Corinthians 11:14** — And no marvel; for Satan himself is transformed into an angel of light.
4. **1 John 2:26,27** (*NKJV*) — These things I have written to you concerning those who try to deceive you. But the anointing which you have received from Him abides in you, and you do not need that anyone teach you; but as the same anointing teaches you concerning all things, and is true, and is not a lie, and just as it has taught you, you will abide in Him.

GREEK WORDS

1. "deceitful" — δόλιος (*dolios*): a word that describes bait put on a hook to catch fish; conveys the idea of craftiness, cheating, cunning, dishonesty, fraud, guile, and trickery intended to entrap someone in an act of deception
2. "workers" — ἐργάτης (*ergates*): denotes someone who actively works at what he is doing or puts great effort into a task
3. "foolish" — ἀνόητος (*anoetos*): brainless, non-thinking people

SYNOPSIS

In Lesson 1, we learned that there are both real and false prophets operating in the world today. Many times, a person can start out with a genuine, God-given gift of prophecy, but over time, it can become corrupted because his or her motives veer off course and become self-centered. When a person increasingly seeks notoriety, influence, or dominance over others, they descend into darkness and error, and the gift of prophecy in their life becomes impure and falsified. To avoid this downfall, we need to stay rooted in God's Word and connected with God's people.

The emphasis of this lesson:

False prophets are cunning, dishonest individuals who fish for gullible people to take their bait and become hooked onto their lies. Like Satan, they work hard at presenting themselves as angels of light to appeal to others and lure them into their web of confusion. Because prophecy is such a valuable gift to God's people in His Kingdom, the enemy tries hard to counterfeit it.

False Prophets Are 'Deceitful Workers'

Paul was a real apostle called by God to bring the Gospel to the Gentiles (*see* Romans 11:13). In various places throughout his writings, he spoke of false apostles and false prophets and warned us of their dangers. The things Paul wrote about false apostles can also apply to false prophets. For example, look at what he said in Second Corinthians 11:13:

> **For such are false apostles, deceitful workers, transforming themselves into the apostles of Christ.**

It is no accident that Paul classified these pretenders as "deceitful workers." What is interesting is that the Greek word for "deceitful" is *dolios*, which is the term used to describe *baiting a hook to catch fish*. Hence, it conveys the idea of *craftiness, cheating, cunning, dishonesty, fraud, guile, and trickery intended to entrap someone in an act of deception.*

Think about what a person does when he fishes. One who is skilled at fishing will cast a baited lure into the water, jerking it every now and then to make the bait look alive. The more alive the lure looks, the more likely the fish will be deceived into taking a bite and becoming hooked. This is how false prophets work.

This brings us to the word "workers," the Greek word *ergates*, which denotes *someone who actively works at what he is doing or puts great effort into a task.* When the Bible joins *dolios* with *ergates* to form the phrase "deceitful workers," it is describing someone who really puts forth a great deal of thought, skill, and effort into cleverly tricking and deceiving people into some sort of trap. Thus, their efforts to deceive are in no way acciden-tal — *they are on purpose.*

Again, the issue here is motivation. In everything that we do, our motive should be to honor and please God and be a blessing to the Body of Christ.

False prophets are deceitful workers who are actively fishing for gullible people that will swallow and be hooked onto their lies. Once their prey has been caught, false prophets can take full advantage of their victims. Here once more, we see the issue of wrong, self-seeking motives. Anyone who is working to prophesy money out of people's pockets and into his own pocket is operating under an impure, falsified gift.

Like Satan, False Prophets Transform Themselves

In the very next verse, the apostle Paul went on to tell us that false prophets operate just like Satan himself. He said:

> **And no marvel; for Satan himself is transformed into an angel of light.**
> — 2 Corinthians 11:14

Just as Satan transforms himself into an angel of light, pretending to be something he's not, false prophets transform themselves into something they are not, something that is appealing to people in order to draw them in. To "transform" means *to transfigure* or *change.* This is a deliberate and intentional metamorphosis someone undergoes to make himself look different than what he really is.

Make no mistake — the reason someone would exert the effort to transform himself into an angel of light is to *purposely* mislead and deceive others to bring them under his influence. This paints the picture of what Paul described as "deceitful workers" in Second Corinthians 11:13. False prophets work extremely hard at making a presentation that is just not authentic.

Don't Just Accept Everything You See and Hear as if It Were From God

The believers in the church at Galatia had fallen prey to such deceitful work-ers, which is why Paul wrote to them and said, "O foolish Galatians, who hath bewitched you, that ye should not obey the truth…" (Galatians 3:1). In the last lesson, we saw that the word "foolish" in this verse is the Greek word *anoetos*, which describes *brainless or non-thinking people*. And we also found the word "bewitched" means *confused*.

The Galatians were bewitched, or confused, because they were not using their brains to think about what they were hearing. The lesson for us to learn here is that we are not to leave our brains at the door and simply receive everything we see and hear someone say because the person saying it claims to be a "prophet." Instead, we have a God-given responsibility to really think about what we are hearing — whether it is a sermon at a church, a prophecy spoken through the Internet, a teaching found on social media, or an experience someone is claiming to have had. We need to judge what we hear against the Word of God and see if it's biblically sound.

Just as you shouldn't eat every physical meal that is placed in front of you, spiritually speaking, you shouldn't eat every ministry meal that comes your way. You need to be mindful of the environment you are in and the source where your spiritual food is coming from. Is it clean and reputable? What kind of track record does the prophet or ministry you're listening to have? Is what you're hearing aligning with God's Word?

The bottom line is that if you don't have peace about what you are hearing or if something doesn't seem right about it, more than likely it is wrong and that prophetic word or teaching should not be received. You are not obligated to eat every spiritual meal that is set in front of you. If it's questionable, you can get up, gather yourself and your family together, and head to a safer eating place.

Satan Seeks To Counterfeit Prophecy Because Real Prophecy Has Great Value

It is important to note that imposters only make knock-off versions of high-quality, name-brand items — they only attempt to imitate things that already have great worth. In the same way, the enemy will not waste his time and energy trying to falsify something that doesn't have value. Prophecy has great value, which is why Satan continues to create a counterfeit version through which he can operate.

This fact seems to apply to what the Holy Spirit prompted the apostle John to write in his first epistle. Here he told all his readers, including us:

> These things I have written to you concerning those who try to deceive you. But the anointing which you have received from Him abides in you, and you do not need that anyone teach you; but as the same anointing teaches you concerning all things, and is true, and is not a lie, and just as it has taught you, you will abide in Him.
>
> — 1 John 2:26,27 (*NKJV*)

Notice it says we have all received an anointing from Jesus. That anointing is His precious Holy Spirit! John declared that the anointing — the Spirit — is true and *not a lie*. The words "not a lie" mean *not phony* or *not false*. John also wrote in his gospel that the Holy Spirit is the Spirit of Truth and will guide us into all truth (*see* John 14:17; 16:13).

Each of us has the anointing of the Holy Spirit living inside us, and if we will pay attention to His leading in our heart, He will enable us to discern what is real and what is false concerning prophetic words we hear as well as direct us in every area of our life. As we abide in relationship with Jesus — feeding on His Word and fellowshipping with His Spirit regularly — we will be able to recognize a false anointing, even an angel of light.

We All Have a Belief System Through Which We See Everything

Another thing that is important to understand is that the way people have been brought up can create issues for them, causing them to either discern or not discern the voice of the Holy Spirit. If they cannot recognize the anointing of the Spirit leading them, they will be unable to receive what He wants them to have or properly navigate what they're experiencing.

As believers, when we perceive something from the realm of the spirit or have a supernatural experience, whether good or bad, we see it through a "shaping filter." Basically, your shaping filter is your *belief system*. To help us understand what a "shaping filter" is, we need to look at what John Wesley called the Wesleyan Quadrilateral. It is made up of four distinct areas:

Scripture

Experiences — The Life of the Believer — Rationality

Tradition

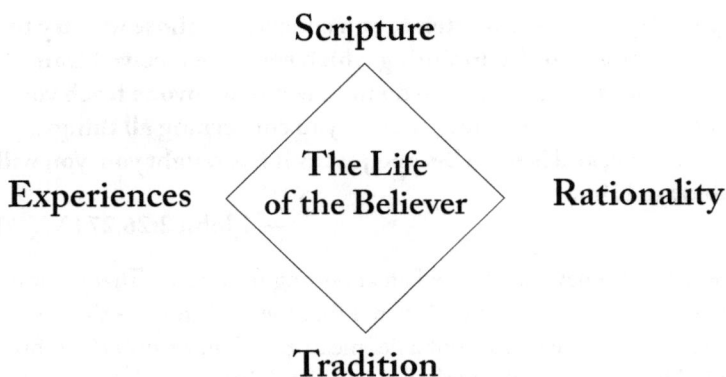

Our "Shaping Filter" — our belief system through which we view the world.

Scripture is what God's Word says about God, others, us, and the world in which we live. Secondly, our *tradition* is what we have been taught by others regarding God's Word, the world, and everything else. Tradition shapes who we are, and it is good as long as it is accurately based on Scripture.

Oftentimes, tradition can clash with Scripture, and as a result, it can cause us to not have good *experiences* when we encounter a true move of the Spirit. Even worse, tradition can sometimes stop good spiritual experiences from happening in our life altogether.

Other factors that come into play and help make up the *experience* part of our "shaping filter," or our belief system, include our environment, the way we were raised, and what we were taught. As a part of our worldview and how we see things, these factors are either going to create a *good, positive* belief system or a *negative* one when we experience things.

Lastly, *rationality* is our ability to mentally and emotionally process Scripture, tradition, and our experiences. It is what we use to properly read the terrain of where we are, where we've been, and where we are heading.

And why is this important? How you view the Word of God and how you process things through your "shaping filter" — your belief system — will determine how and what you are able to receive from the realm of the spirit. For instance, if an "angel of light" manifests in your life or you experience something bizarre in the realm of the spirit, if you're someone who loves the sensational and is easily carried away by crazy encounters, and you're *not* rooted in God's Word, you will likely be deceived.

Of course, the Lord doesn't want you to be deceived, which is why Jesus warns in Matthew 24:4, "…Take heed that no man deceive you." Instead, He wants you to live and walk in the full counsel of God. This comes in the form of revelation, interpretation, and application of truth in your life.

Understanding what specific things make up your belief system is a major key to ensure you interpret and apply things correctly to receive the very best from God and avoid the trap of deception.

Being Rooted in God's Word Gives Us Protection Against Deception

Now you may be wondering, *Why do angels of light come? Why do demonic influences and entities show up through the lives of people who are under their influence and try to connect in those ways?* The primary reason these ungodly forces try to interact with us is to deceive us and thereby gain access to operate through us in the natural realm.

The fact is that we are all *gatekeepers* or *agents of permission* who exist between the natural realm and the spiritual realm. Demonic entities are real and are constantly trying to influence us directly or indirectly through others, and if our belief system is flawed and these evil entities get us to agree with something that is wrong spiritually, they can gain access to our lives and work through us to deceive and influence others also.

Think about the leaders who started various cults. Most of them had some type of supernatural experience that greatly impacted them, but their experience was not based on Scripture. In many cases, what happened was also totally irrational and outside of sound teaching or Bible-based tradition. Therefore, nothing in their belief system was able to correct or stand against the spiritual deception that came against them.

Hebrews 5:14 says, "But strong meat belongeth to them that are of full age, even those who by reason of use have their senses exercised to discern both good and evil." The words "strong meat" refers to Scripture. When you are spiritually mature, your soul and spirit are filled with God's Word, and your senses are exercised and able to discern what is good and what is evil. In other words, when you are deeply rooted in the Word of God, it is much harder for you to be deceived — even by an angel of light.

The Word of God makes you smart in every area. If you are grounded in the Word, it won't take you long to figure out if something is wrong or right.

You will know it instinctively. Jesus is the Word of God (*see* John 1:1), and the more of the Word you have in you, the more of Jesus you have in you. Being rooted in God's Word is powerful protection against deception.

If you will read the Bible long enough, it will start talking back to you. The Holy Spirit who authored every word will begin to use it in your life to adjust and shape your thoughts, your feelings, your decisions, and your convictions — and before you know it, you will be doing what the Word of God says and walking in the Spirit with ease.

Experiences Should Always Take a Backseat to God's Word

Many people are struggling from the effects of bad teaching, and as a result, they emphasize experiences over God's Word. If some would-be prophet ever tells you to set your mind aside or set aside the Word of God and "just believe what they are saying," *don't do it!* Anything that is genuinely of the Lord can be processed and understood with your mind because it is backed up by Scripture, and Scripture is the sure foundation for our Christian life.

God gave us our minds, and as believers, we should be the smartest and sharpest people on the planet! If someone is teaching, preaching, or prophesying something that is from the Lord, it will line up with Scripture and bring you peace in your spirit. God is not the author of confusion, and He does everything decently and in order (*see* 1 Corinthians 14:33,40). The more you know the Word, the more you will know whether something is of God or not.

STUDY QUESTIONS

Study to shew thyself approved unto God, a workman that needeth not to be ashamed, rightly dividing the word of truth.
— 2 Timothy 2:15

1. One of the best ways to know whether something is of God is to be still and see if you have peace in your heart about it. Having an inner peace about what you're hearing, what you're doing, or a decision you're about to make is often the greatest seal of approval from God. Take time to meditate on this amazing passage in Colossians 3:15

(*AMPC*) and write down what the Holy Spirit reveals to you about the value and importance of God's peace:

And let the peace (soul harmony which comes) from Christ rule (act as umpire continually) in your hearts [deciding and settling with finality all questions that arise in your minds, in that peaceful state] to which as [members of Christ's] one body you were also called [to live]. And be thankful (appreciative), [giving praise to God always].

2. To keep us from being deceived, God has given us the truth of His Word and His amazing Holy Spirit. Do you know the primary roles the Holy Spirit is called to fulfill in your life? Look up these passages to learn what an extraordinary gift the Spirit is meant to be for you!

   • John 6:63; Romans 8:11; Second Corinthians 3:6

   • John 14:16,26; 16:13-15

   • Luke 12:11,12; First John 2:20,27

PRACTICAL APPLICATION

> But be ye doers of the word, and not hearers only,
> deceiving your own selves.
> —James 1:22

1. As a believer, when you see or hear something from the realm of the spirit — or you have a supernatural experience, whether good or bad — you see it through a "shaping filter." This is your *belief system* that's filtered through four aspects. Take a few moments to pray and ask the Holy Spirit to give you some understanding of how these four areas have developed in your life and how they are presently functioning.

Scripture: _____

_____

Tradition: _____

_____

Experiences: _____

_____

Rationality: _____

2. When you're deeply rooted in the Word of God, it is much harder to be deceived — even by an angel of light. The Word makes you smart in every area. Be honest — how important and valuable is God's Word to you? Take an inventory of how much time and effort you invest in reading and studying Scripture. Does it reflect a genuine appreciation for God's Word? What can you remove from your daily routine so you can have more time with the Holy Spirit to reveal to you the hidden treasures of Scripture?

TOPIC

Judging Prophecy and Dealing With Prophetic Mistakes

SCRIPTURES

1. **1 Thessalonians 5:19,20** — Quench not the Spirit. Despise not prophesyings.
2. **1 Thessalonians 5:21** — Prove all things; hold fast that which is good.
3. **2 Thessalonians 2:2** — That ye be not soon shaken in mind, or be troubled, neither by spirit, nor by word, nor by letter as from us, as that the day of Christ is at hand.

GREEK WORDS

"despise" — ἐξουθενέω (*exoutheneo*): to look down on, to disdain, or to ridicule

SYNOPSIS

Everyone makes mistakes — even those who love God, have the best of intentions, and walk in integrity. The good news is that just because someone may make a mistake in operating in the gift of prophecy doesn't mean that person is false — it just means that person is human and has room to grow. In this lesson, we will focus on the right way and wrong way of responding to prophetic mistakes.

The emphasis of this lesson:

As believers, we're not to discard the gift of prophecy simply because people have made mistakes or abused the gift. Instead, we're to use wisdom as we listen to and receive prophetic messages and when we give them out as prompted by the Spirit of God. Knowing that depth perception as well as feelings and desires can cause a person to prophesy incorrectly, our words must be chosen carefully and spoken humbly.

Don't Despise or Discard Prophecy Because of a Bad Experience

Both First and Second Thessalonians were written by the apostle Paul, and one of the reasons he wrote these letters to believers was because someone in the church at Thessalonica was misusing the gift of prophecy. Whether it was deliberate or a mistake is irrelevant — the fact is that the misuse of prophecy was creating a mess.

In response to being burned by what took place, the Thessalonian believers were opting to throw out the prophetic gift and prevent it from occurring in their gatherings. But that was a foolish overreaction. It would be the equivalent of someone saying, "I had a good friend that was in a tragic car accident, and because of what happened to them, I'm not getting in another car."

Do you see the absurdity in such a statement? We don't throw away all cars because we or someone we know was in a bad accident. We simply make sure that the car in which we are traveling is driven safely. In the same way, we don't throw away the gift of prophecy because of a bad experience. Instead, we simply learn to use wisdom when listening to and receiving prophetic messages and to judge them by the safe guidelines of the Word of God. That is what Paul was instructing the Thessalonian believers to do when he wrote:

Quench not the Spirit.

— 1 Thessalonians 5:19

Essentially, in verse 19, Paul was saying, "Don't damper or extinguish the movement of the Holy Spirit among you." He then specifically added:

Despise not prophesyings.
— 1 Thessalonians 5:20

The word "despise" here is the Greek word *exoutheneo*, which means *to look down on, to disdain*, or *to ridicule*. Because there had been several prophetic mistakes, the Thessalonians were looking down on and disdaining the gift of prophecy — and many people in our day have done the same thing because of prophecies that were spoken but didn't come to pass. But, again, a bad experience with the prophetic does not negate the value of all prophecies and prophetic teaching.

'Prove All Prophetic Things'

What Paul said then still applies to us now. Rather than throw everything away just because of a bad experience, he urged believers not to despise or ridicule the prophetic, and to:

Prove all things; hold fast that which is good.
— 1 Thessalonians 5:21

The instruction to "prove all things" is basically Paul's way of saying, "Use your head! If you were duped, it's because you weren't thinking. The next time a prophetic word comes forth, judge it against Scripture. Then hold fast to what is good." The fact is, there is a great deal of prophetic ministry that is really good, and if you avoid or throw away the prophetic, you will miss out on things that the Spirit of God wants to say to the Body of Christ.

God gave us the fivefold ministry gifts, which include prophecy and the office of the prophet, because He knows we need it. The devil wants people to focus on prophetic mistakes, get discouraged, and discard the prophetic altogether. But if we did that, there would be an entire aspect of Christ missing from the Church.

Bizarre Prophetic Claims Are Happening Now Just as They Were in the Early Church

It is interesting to note that when we come to Second Thessalonians 2, we see that the problem with the prophetic that Paul tried to address in his first letter to the Thessalonians did not go away. There were still mistakes being made. In fact, it appears that a well-known person in the church had begun to prophesy that the Rapture had already taken place and the remaining believers had missed it. The person who made this claim must have been very notable and respected because virtually everyone believed it and was deeply disturbed.

To set the record straight and release peace to their minds and hearts, Paul wrote:

> **That ye be not soon shaken in mind, or be troubled, neither by spirit, nor by word, nor by letter as from us, as that the day of Christ is at hand.**
> — **2 Thessalonians 2:2**

When we insert the original Greek meaning of the words in this verse, the *Renner Interpretive Version* (*RIV*) of Second Thessalonians 2:2 says:

> **I also want to tell you not to be too surprised if people start making weird spiritual proclamations and off-the-wall utterances during the time just before the Lord comes. All kinds of strange things are going to happen during those days. It's going to get so bizarre that you might even receive a letter from some person who claims the day of the Lord has already come. Who knows? They might even attach our name to it, alleging to have our endorsement, or they might even send it as if it were written from us.**

Isn't it interesting that nearly 2,000 years ago, Paul wrote and told believers that weird spiritual proclamations and off-the-wall utterances would be made during the time just before the Lord comes. And these bizarre claims would be spoken "in the name of prophecy." This is very similar to what we are dealing with today.

Therefore, we need to keep our head on straight and use our God-given intellect to understand if what is being said aligns with Scripture and if it is of God or not. By using our head, we won't become bewitched and confused.

Strong Desires and Emotions
Can Cause a Prophet To Make Mistakes

Sometimes well-meaning people prophesy what they *want* to happen instead of prophesying what the Lord says. Other times, they prophesy out of the overflow of their emotions, or they prophesy their own doctrine. It's okay to prophesy one's doctrine — as long as it's good, biblical doctrine.

Joseph Z clarifies, "There's a saying we have that goes like this, 'If you torture the data long enough, you can make it confess to anything.'" In other words, if you're obsessed over an issue, and you really want to see something turn out a certain way, eventually your desires and feelings can overtake you and supersede the prophetic voice. Prophetic people can be guilty of this, because as humans, we know in part, and we prophesy in part (*see* 1 Corinthians 13:9).

When we read the Bible and interpret what it says, we don't have the right to make it say what we want it to say. To be true to Scripture, we must interpret the words and phrases for what they *actually say*, and the same principle applies to prophecy. A prophet, or anyone who prophesies, doesn't have the right to inject what he wants to say in the message the Lord has given him or to interpret what he thinks He meant. The prophet is speaking on the Lord's behalf, and he must speak clearly what He has said.

Depth Perception Can Also Be a Challenge
for Prophesying Accurately

Many times, people who are gifted in the prophetic see things that are coming, and the vision they have is accurate. The problem is that what they are seeing may be what is about to happen next week — *or it may be what is going to take place next year or even in the distant future.*

"It's called depth perception," says Joseph Z. "This is always an issue with speaking prophetically. When we see things in the realm of the spirit, it is very difficult to know if what we're seeing is for *right now* or *down the road*. I believe that is what happened in the last few years when people predicted some of the political outcomes that didn't take place."

For many prophetic people, it is like the Lord downloads a spiritual map right in front of them, and as they read the map, they begin to prophesy and say things like, "The Lord showed me this is what is going to happen. And once this event takes place, this person is going to get into office." But then time passes, and what they perceived doesn't take place.

Make no mistake. They have certainly seen something, and it's strong in their heart. Eventually, after much time has passed, something will likely begin to manifest. But while it may be similar to what the Lord showed this prophet, what actually takes place is different than what they saw.

Joseph Z explains, "The spiritual map is God's *revelation*; time brings the *interpretation*; and the *application* is given by the Spirit once the prophecy becomes reality."

"This challenge of depth perception," Rick says, "is the reason it is so important for those who are speaking in the name of the Lord to preface what they say with words like, *'I perceive,' 'I feel,'* or *'I sense.'* The reality is that sometimes what we see turns out a little different than what we prophesied."

What Are We To Do When
the Spiritual Map Differs From the Terrain?

As believers, the Word of God is our road map, and when we see something in the Bible, we are to stand on it and do it, no matter what we see coming next. But when it comes to seeing something prophetic in the realm of the spirit and then acting on it, things are a little different.

There was a mathematician named Korzybski who said that when you are studying things, the map and the actual territory may differ. Spiritually speaking, when a person sees something in the spirit that's coming, it's kind of like a spiritual map that the Lord gives to those who operate in the prophetic.

When God allows His prophets to see a coming event, the vision is the *map*. They then declare, "This is what is coming." But when it finally arrives and manifests in real time, it is often different. The reason for this is because the spiritual map only provides a limited view of what is about to happen. When the prophesied event finally takes place, it is a much more detailed, 3-D *terrain*, which must be navigated because that is what is currently happening.

"When the map and the terrain differ," Joseph Z says, "We are to read the terrain. In other words, when the prophecy that the Spirit of the Lord gives us and the actual manifestation of that prophecy differs, we need to focus our attention and efforts on reading and understanding the real-time manifestation."

Let's say you are studying a map to see all the different roads you are going to need to take on an upcoming trip. On the map, the representation of the roads appear one way, but when you are driving and you come to the actual road or intersection you saw on the map, it often looks very different. At that point, navigating the road in front of you supersedes the importance of the map.

Spiritually speaking, it is the same. When the Holy Spirit enables a person to perceive something in the spirit realm, it's like they are given a map, and they have a sense about what's coming. But then when the actual event takes place, it may be different than what the person saw. The depth perception of time might produce something different.

This is why it's important to focus on reading and navigating the real-time manifestation of the prophecy. When the spiritual map, *the prophecy*, differs from the terrain, *the actual manifestation* of that prophecy — we need to read the terrain. We need to be fully aware of what is happening around us and prayerfully navigate our real-time circumstances and situations. This is where knowing the Bible and using common sense comes in.

Now, there are some prophetic people that get upset when the prophecy they received manifests differently than what they saw. They may say things like, "Wait a second! This is different than what I predicted." And rather than adjust to what is actually happening, they cling tenaciously to the prophetic word they received and possibly shared with others.

This is where humility comes in. Everyone operating in the prophetic must admit that when God is showing them something, "…We know in part, and we prophesy in part" (1 Corinthians 13:9).

Sometimes the Prophecy Can Be Accurate But the Timing May Be Off

Maybe you remember that during a previous U.S. presidential election cycle, there were prophetic voices who were saying a certain candidate was going to win. And some of these well-meaning, anointed prophets, whom we greatly love and respect, began to give specific details as to what was going to take place. But when election night came and went, the candidate that was prophesied to win actually lost, and things didn't play out as many had predicted. This left many people in the Body of Christ very confused and disillusioned.

Some of these prophetic voices continued to declare that this particular candidate did win, but he won "in the spirit." Others claimed that there were problems with the voting process in various states. What really happened, only God knows. But publicly, in whatever manner was used to decide the outcome, this candidate was not elected to office.

In a situation like this, what should happen is that those who prophesied something that didn't happen as they predicted should humble themselves and say, "I believe I saw something regarding this person, but maybe what I saw is for a future time."

Prophecy and Scripture Often Have a Much Deeper, Fuller Meaning

Often, when we read something in Scripture or something is seen in the realm of the spirit, there is a much deeper, fuller meaning to the vision than what is initially seen. The Latin word for this is called *sensus plenior*, which literally means "fuller sense" or "deeper meaning."

As we said earlier, depth perception can certainly be a challenge for those operating in the gift of prophecy. What a prophet perceives can be accurate, but their interpretation of the timing of the event — as well as the depth of its meaning — can be incorrect.

On the program, Rick shared how many years ago, when he was just starting out in ministry, he experienced a moment when he saw into the realm of the spirit and was given a picture of several things the Lord would use him to do in ministry. It was so real and vivid, he thought it was going to take place immediately. Therefore, he did everything he could to make those things happen, but nothing worked.

Decades later, what Rick previously perceived himself to be doing was actually taking place in the present, which confirmed that what he had sensed in the spirit all those years ago was accurate. But because of the challenge of spiritual depth perception, his timing was wrong.

It could be that the Lord doesn't allow us to have a full, detailed picture of what is coming and the timing of its arrival so that we will remain humbly focused on Him and not on the prophecy. As we continue to seek His face and submit to one another in unity, He will add clarity and detail to the prophecies He is communicating when it's the right time.

Choosing Our Words Carefully
Guards the Reputation of God and the Prophetic

A sad tragedy is when God's people criticize prophetic voices that are trying to decipher and navigate what the Lord is showing them in the realm of the spirit. Equally sad is when a prophetic person sees something they have said is incorrect, and they won't admit it. Again, this is why walking in humility is so vital.

When a person makes a "Thus saith the Lord" statement, and they are not rock-solid sure about the details and the timing of it, they trap themselves with their words. Then when the prophecy fails to take place as predicted, they are labeled by others as a false prophet, and the gift of prophecy is disdained and ridiculed.

Instead of making a rigid proclamation that something is absolutely going to take place, a good practice for all of us to have when sharing something we perceive from the Lord is to say:

> "This is what I am *sensing* and *perceiving* in my spirit. I'm not really sure of all the details yet, so you judge it and pray about it for yourself."

We get a sense of this kind of humble communication in Acts 15 where the apostles wrote to the new Gentile believers and shared with them what they felt the Lord required. They said, "For *it seemed good* to the Holy Ghost, and to us, to lay upon you no greater burden than these necessary things" (Acts 15:28). As Early Church leaders were in fellowship with each other and the Holy Spirit, they collectively had a general sense of what the Lord wanted, and they shared what they sensed by saying "it seemed good" which revealed an attitude of humility.

Always remember that words are expensive. In other words, saying the wrong thing can be costly. *Lord, help us get a heart-revelation of this truth! Help us humbly and carefully choose our words and save ourselves and others from much heartache.*

A Prophetic Word of Blessing

Have you ever been deeply disappointed or burned by a bad prophetic experience? Don't let that cause you to throw away the gift of prophecy. Remember, if there is a counterfeit, there is also a real. Although the person who spoke on behalf of God may have made an honest mistake and was incorrect in their interpretation, the Spirit of God is never wrong and doesn't make mistakes.

If you've been led down a road that left you hurt or affected your faith in the Lord, God wants to restore life to you right now! We bless you, in Jesus' name, and pray His peace, His hope, and supernatural order is imparted into your heart right now. We speak healing to every wound and remove every arrow the enemy has shot at you in the form of wrong words that were spoken. May God's goodness, mercy, favor, and love be released into your life right now, in Jesus' name!

Friend, God loves you, and Jesus wants you to experience the pure gift of prophecy. We bless you with clear-eyed, clear-minded breakthrough, in Jesus' name. Remember, no matter what is going on, God is always speaking, and if you will lean into His Spirit, you will hear His voice. Let go of the old and step into the new. God is with you!

STUDY QUESTIONS

> Study to shew thyself approved unto God, a workman that
> needeth not to be ashamed, rightly dividing the word of truth.
> — 2 Timothy 2:15

1. Although not all of us operate in the office of a prophet, as devoted sons or daughters of God, we are sometimes enabled to see a glimpse of things that are coming so that we can be prepared. To help you better understand the prophetic insight God has made available to you, read these passages and write what the Holy Spirit reveals to you.

   • Amos 3:7

   • Psalm 25:14

   • Daniel 2:20-23

   • John 15:15; 16:13 and First Corinthians 2:9,10

2. *Humility* is an important virtue for all believers to walk in — not just for those who are prophets. How important and powerful is humility? Look at what God says about it in these key verses:
   - James 4:6; First Peter 5:5; and Proverbs 3:34
   - Proverbs 22:4; 29:23
   - Matthew 18:4; 23:12 and Luke 14:11; 18:14
   - Philippians 2:3-8 and James 4:10

PRACTICAL APPLICATION

But be ye doers of the word, and not hearers only,
deceiving your own selves.
—James 1:22

1. In this lesson, we learned about the challenges of depth perception in prophecy and how a person's strong feelings and desires can often influence and even redirect the accuracy of a prophecy. How do these eye-opening truths help you better understand why a prophecy can be incorrect?

   On the program, Rick candidly shared how when he was starting out in ministry, he had a prophetic vision of how God was going to use him, but what he saw didn't happen until decades later. Have you ever experienced a situation like this? If so, what did God show you in advance? How long was it before it became a reality? What lessons has the Holy Spirit taught you through this experience?

2. The enemy wants us to focus on prophetic mistakes, get discouraged, and discard the prophetic altogether. If you've been hurt by prophetic voices, take some time now to pray. Tell God how you feel and invite the Holy Spirit to help you surrender your disappointment, frustration, and even anger over what took place. Then ask Him to heal your heart so that you can be open to the prophetic gift once again.

TOPIC

Rightsizing the Prophetic

SCRIPTURES

1. **1 Thessalonians 5:12** — And we beseech you, brethren, to know them which labour among you, and are over you in the Lord, and admonish you.
2. **1 Corinthians 15:46** — Howbeit that was not first which is spiritual, but that which is natural; and afterward that which is spiritual.
3. **2 Corinthians 10:3** — For though we walk in the flesh....
4. **John 6:63** — It is the spirit that quickeneth; the flesh profiteth nothing: the words that I speak unto you, they are spirit, and they are life.
5. **1 Chronicles 12:32** — And of the children of Issachar, which were men that had understanding of the times, to know what Israel ought to do; the heads of them were two hundred; and all their brethren were at their commandment.

GREEK WORDS

"beseech" — ἐρωτάω (*erotao*): to plead; to make an earnest request

SYNOPSIS

In recent years, there have been some individuals who have given prophetic words that didn't come to pass exactly as they predicted, and as a result, many have lost confidence in the fivefold office of the prophet. The truth is, all of us make mistakes — including God's leaders. And just because someone was a little inaccurate or had a bad depth perception, it doesn't mean all prophecy is false.

Indeed, there is great value in prophecy, otherwise Satan wouldn't perpetually attack it and try to pervert it. Rather than despise or scoff at the gift of prophecy, we should "...test everything that is said. Hold on to what is good. Stay away from every kind of evil" (1 Thessalonians 5:21,22 *NLT*). In this hour, God is enabling His remnant to rightsize the ministry of the prophetic.

The emphasis of this lesson:

Rightsizing the prophetic means bringing the office of the prophet back into proper alignment according to the Bible so that those who flow in the prophetic will function at optimal levels. To see this happen, those who operate in prophetic ministry must be accurately trained in God's Word and they must stay in a submitted relationship with like-minded, fivefold ministry leaders.

Get To Know and Understand
Who Is Speaking Into Your Life

Looking again at Paul's letter to the believers in Thessalonica, he wrote, "...We beseech you, brethren, to know them which labour among you, and are over you in the Lord, and admonish you" (1 Thessalonians 5:12). In this passage, the word "beseech" is a translation of the Greek word *erotao*, and it means *to plead* or *to make an earnest request.*

Essentially, Paul was urging and pleading with early believers, and us, to learn about the people who were working in and around their environment. Of course, this includes our pastors, elders, deacons, and other church leaders and members, but this principle can also be applied to individuals laboring outside the Church.

Rick shared on the program how he familiarizes himself with the reporters who bring him the news:

> I really like to know who's talking to me, even when I'm watching the news. If a brand-new correspondent comes on to give a report, I immediately take my computer, which is usually near me because I'm writing all the time, and I go online to find out who the reporter is.

> I search for details like: Where did they go to school? Who taught them? Who do they run with? And what is their political persuasion? All these dynamics affect the way they're going to report the news.

> These facts will also help me know what kind of predetermined bias they may bring as they deliver the news. It will also help me know if I can trust them. Again, I do all this because I want to know who is giving me the news.

News reporters are not the only people Rick investigates. He applies a similar, if not more rigorous, scrutiny to the authors of the books he reads and the teachers he watches online.

> In the very same way, if I am about to read a book or watch someone on television or the Internet and I don't know who they are, but they're interesting to me, before I embrace them, I do a little study to check out their background. I want to know who is speaking.
>
> In this case, I try to determine things like: Where did they go to Bible school? Do they have any Bible education? Who do they run with? Do I agree with the philosophies of the people in their circles? Are they submitted to authority? And do they attend a church?
>
> All of these factors are going to determine whether or not I'm going to read a person's book or listen to them teach, and I encourage you to do the same thing.
>
> You need to know who is speaking and ministering to you through social media, YouTube, television, radio, and books. You need to be aware of who they are and what they're about *before* you open your heart to them. If you'll take the time to check them out beforehand, it might save you a lot of pain and misery.

The background and character of the people you watch and listen to will impact and influence you. Patterns determine capacity. If an individual you are allowing to speak into your life did something before and then did it a second or third time, more than likely, they will do it again. This principle is true in both the secular as well as the Christian world.

When it comes to prophetic ministry, if someone has been really erroneous and made terrible mistakes before, they will probably do it again. On the contrary, if someone has been humble, positive, and they've really hit the mark again and again, more than likely they will continue in the same way. That person would probably be a voice you want to listen to.

What Does 'Rightsizing the Prophetic' Mean?

To "rightsize" something in this context means to put something back into its proper place. Hence, when we talk about "rightsizing the prophetic," we are talking about bringing the office of the prophet back into proper alignment according to the Word of God so that those who flow in the prophetic will function at optimal levels.

One of the most important keys to doing that is for those who operate in this gift to stay in a submitted relationship with like-minded, fivefold ministry leaders. This holds true for apostles, prophets, evangelists, pastors, and teachers.

Again, when it comes to the ministry leaders you listen to, to whom are they accountable? Who talks to them about their life? Are there godly leaders cautioning them to choose their words carefully? If they're not in relationship with seasoned, godly people that have a right to speak into their life, then it would probably not be wise to listen to them.

Prophets and prophetic people can do the Body of Christ a great service. They have helped the Church quite a bit, but there is much more that they could do, which is why we are talking about rightsizing the prophetic.

It seems in recent times that prophetic ministry has been like a sailboat that's been tipped over on its side as it makes its way through the sea. In this lopsided position, it is not nearly as effective as it could be. However, if we can help to rightsize it, bringing it back into its proper position, we can optimize its usefulness and strength. It appears that the Lord is presently doing this to help us better understand prophetic ministry.

When prophetic people see into the realm of the spirit, they are not always accurate. Their level of accuracy really depends on how they were trained in Scripture and who they're in relationship with to keep them accountable.

Being trained in the Word is extremely important for those who are operating in the prophetic. Inspirational words are helpful, but they will only go so far. Prophetic ministers need eternal substance to what they say, and that can only come from the Word of God. When you are a prophetic person that has a strong foundation of Scripture, you are much less likely to make prophetic mistakes.

There Is a Natural Realm and a Spirit Realm

Imagine a circle on a piece of paper. Now, imagine that a line is drawn down the middle. The right half of the circle represents the natural, physical realm in which we live, and the left half of the circle represents the realm of the spirit — the dimension we cannot see. And the line between the two halves represents the veil that separates the natural realm from the spirit realm.

Interestingly, First Corinthians 15:46 (*NLT*) says, "What comes first is the natural body, then the spiritual body comes later." The biblical principle here is that the *natural* realm is first, *then* the spirit realm. Although some people claim that as soon as they open their eyes in the morning, they wake up in the realm of the spirit and immediately begin communicating with God, that is not the case. Every person wakes up in the natural realm, no matter how long they've been walking with the Lord or how close they feel to Him.

The Bible confirms this in Second Corinthians 10:3, where it says, "…We walk in the flesh…." Indeed, we are flesh and blood creatures who live in the natural realm. At the same time, we are also spirit beings, but to get into the realm of the spirit, we must purposely do something to navigate there.

If you wake up in the morning and you don't feel the power of God and sense all the fruit of the Spirit flowing freely through you, you are not alone. If we are honest, no one wakes up that way. We all wake up in this natural, fallen world, and in order to get into the realm of the spirit, we need to activate our faith by obeying what God says in His Word and step into the spirit realm by tuning our hearts to His voice.

Acting on God's Word in the Natural Triggers a Supernatural Response in the Spirit

Now when it comes to the area of the prophetic, moving into the realm of the spirit is very important. Jesus said, "God is a Spirit: and they that worship him must worship him in spirit and in truth" (John 4:24). It is in the realm of the spirit where real truth is and the greater reality is found. The problem is that there is a veil separating the two realms. How do we clearly hear God's voice and accurately bring what He is saying into the natural?

We need to act in faith in the natural, doing what God's Word says.

As we obey God's Word and apply it to our lives and in our natural situations, something extraordinary happens. A great example of the way this works is seen in healing. God's Word says, "Is any sick among you? let him call for the elders of the church; and let them pray over him, anointing him with oil in the name of the Lord" (James 5:14).

When we obediently act on God's Word in the natural realm, something happens in the realm of the spirit. The very next verse says, "And the prayer of faith shall save the sick, and the Lord shall raise him up..." (v.15).

When a physical action is carried out, a supernatural, spiritual reaction is produced.

The natural action of laying hands on a sick person and praying triggers a supernatural reaction in the spirit realm that manifests back in the natural realm. Healing is experienced!

This principle also works with salvation. God's Word says, "...If you confess with your mouth the Lord Jesus and believe in your heart that God has raised Him from the dead, you will be saved" (Romans 10:9 *NKJV*). When you obey God's Word and say a prayer in the natural, it triggers a supernatural reaction in the spirit realm that manifests back in the natural. You are saved!

Now, when we apply this principle to the area of prophecy, to accurately hear the voice of the Lord, we need to sharpen our soul. The Bible says, "...We know in part, and we prophesy in part," (1 Corinthians 13:9) and "For now we see through a glass, darkly..." (v.12). As we sharpen our soul — our mind, will, and emotions — we will begin to clearly perceive the things of the spirit. We do this by meditating on the Word of God and praying in the spirit.

Praying in Tongues Brings You Into the Realm of the Spirit

The first way to access the realm of the spirit is through knowing and speaking God's Word. In John 6:63, Jesus said, "...The words that I speak unto you, they are *spirit*, and they are life." So, the fact that we have the Word of God, means we have a connection with the realm of the spirit.

Equally important is the fact that we are the temple, or house, in which the Holy Spirit lives (*see* 1 Corinthians 3:16; 6:19). To activate the unction, or anointing, of the Spirit, we are to pray in the language of the spirit. This is what the Bible calls *tongues*. By far, this is the best way to sharpen one's soul because praying in tongues bypasses the natural mind. Many times, we don't know what to pray from our natural intellect — especially when weighed down with challenging situations. For example, let's say we are thinking and praying about our spouse, our children, our job, or our finances with our natural mind. Naturally, human logic and emotions will emerge and try to confine our prayers to the realm of the natural.

In contrast, when we pray in the spirit, our natural mind is pushed out of the equation. It is our spirit man praying directly to the Spirit of God in a language our mind cannot understand (*see* 1 Corinthians 14:2). Praying in tongues is the most powerful and intimate communication we can have with God because it enables us as believers to talk directly with Him on the deepest level — *spirit to Spirit*.

To hear the things of the Spirit, you must move in and pray in the spirit. The longer and more frequently you pray in your prayer language — in tongues — the more you are transported into the realm of the spirit and have access to all the amazingly good things that are there. Then what is happening in the spirit will begin to manifest in your soul, bringing order, peace, and power to every area of your life.

Entering the Realm of the Spirit Enabled Rick To Receive Needed Revelation

To help us get a picture of how praying in tongues enables us to access the realm of the spirit, Rick openly shared this story on the program about a time when he was walking through some challenges, and he really didn't even want to pray:

> I had an experience many years ago — one I rarely share. I felt that I needed to pray, have the Lord speak to me, and really get a breakthrough. So I went to the back room of the house where we were staying and got real still.

> Honestly, I didn't feel like praying. I was really stuck in the natural realm, focused on all the things we were dealing with at the time.

> But despite how I was feeling, I made the choice to begin praying in tongues, and before long, I began to experience the realm of the spirit, just like we've been describing in this teaching.

As I prayed in tongues, I began to dip into the spirit and then come back into my natural thinking. Back and forth I went — praying in the spirit and then with understanding, just like the apostle Paul talks about in First Corinthians 14:15.

I prayed in tongues and prayed in tongues and prayed in tongues until finally I felt myself getting lost in tongues. I had dipped down so deep into the realm of the spirit that when I opened my eyes, even though I was physically still in that room, I did not see the room. I was standing in another dimension where God began to reveal things to me.

Looking back, I know that had I not made that choice in the natural to pray in tongues and begin to dip down into the realm of the spirit, I would have never received the revelation I needed.

Rick's story is a great example of accessing the spirit realm and obtaining the things he needed that he couldn't get anywhere else. His solid, biblical foundation allowed him to remain stable through his supernatural experience and not veer off track into spiritual error like some who've had such encounters have done.

Find Your 'Tribe' and Stay With Them

In addition to knowing and speaking God's Word and praying in the language of your spirit, it is also very important to find like-minded and like-gifted people with whom you can walk closely in company with. Joseph Z describes this as "finding your tribe" and sticking with them.

Basically, a "tribe" is the group of people you know in your heart God has placed you with, whom you have a heart connection with and can fellowship with on a regular basis. These are fellow believers in the Body of Christ who are called by God to serve and connect in the same areas of life and ministry in which you are called to be in this season.

The sons of Issachar is a great example of what a tribe looks like. They are mentioned in First Chronicles 12:32, which says that the sons of Issachar "…were men that had understanding of the times, to know what Israel ought to do; the heads of them were two hundred; and all their brethren were at their commandment."

In today's world, there are many prophetic voices that know and understand the signs of the times. Not only do they tell you what's going on, but they also tell you what to do about it. The problem, however, is that they are disjointed in the Body of Christ — they are disconnected from their tribe.

When you are with the right people — your tribe — you become rightly aligned in your life. As a result, order and strength come to what God is showing you. Likewise, when you're with the right people, you are more effective and can live in a greater degree of freedom because you can be who you authentically are. Also amazing is that you see things very similarly as you are each in God's Word.

Now, you may ask, "How do I know if I'm with the right people — my tribe?" Well, one way you can tell is that if you're with the right people, you can't say the wrong thing to them. What that means is that if you are with your tribe, they will understand your heart, and even if you say something that's incorrect or a little out of place, they won't judge you inappropriately.

The other side of that is if you are with the wrong people, it seems like you can never say the right thing to them. The wrong people — those who are *not* your tribe — will only tolerate you, not celebrate you. Of course, if you are in rebellion and not listening to the things of God, that is a different story. You need to repent and get yourself in order.

How Are We To Judge the Prophetic?

Some people say, "You shouldn't judge! Even Jesus said, 'Judge not, that ye be not judged' (Matthew 7:1)." That's true. Jesus did say that, but the judging He is talking about here is being *judgmental* and critical of others. There is a difference between making a judgment call about something and being judgmental.

The fact is we are judging things all the time. Another word we might use is evaluate. We judge whether to put our hand in fire and evaluate if we will get burned. We also judge whether to walk out in the middle of traffic and evaluate if we will get hit by a car. There's nothing wrong with this kind of judging because it is basically evaluating something to determine if the thought or words being projected have a stable foundation.

When it comes to rightsizing the prophetic, we are not to be judgmental of the people we are listening to because that doesn't help anyone. However, God does want us to use our minds to judge if what we are hearing is truly from Him. In fact, the Bible exhorts us to judge the prophetic when it says, "Despise not prophesyings. *Prove* all things; hold fast that which is good" (1 Thessalonians 5:20,21).

So friend, use wisdom and know what the Bible says on issues that pertain to life and godliness. Then you will be able to judge with discernment what you are hearing. When you know something is from God, take time to thank Him and appreciate that He has spoken to you prophetically through another brother or sister. Indeed, the gift of prophecy is meant to be a great blessing to you and the entire Body of Christ!

STUDY QUESTIONS

Study to shew thyself approved unto God, a workman that needeth not to be ashamed, rightly dividing the word of truth.
— 2 Timothy 2:15

1. Having a strong foundation in God's Word is essential to hearing the voice of the Holy Spirit as you seek the Lord. King David wrote in the Psalms that God's Word was a light to his path (*see* Psalm 119:105). Which scriptures stand out to you as ones that help govern your walk with the Lord so you can stay on the correct path? Consider Psalm 37:4-11, Proverbs 4:20-26, Galatians 5:19-24, and Ephesians 4:17-32. Are there other scriptures that have really helped you grow further in your walk with the Lord?

2. On the program, Rick and Joseph Z both mentioned the importance of praying in tongues, which again is simply praying in your prayer language. Read the following scriptures to discover the value and benefits of having your own personal prayer language in which to communicate with the Lord and pray out the perfect plan of God for your own life.

   - Luke 11:9-13

   - Acts 1:4-8; 19:1-6

   - Romans 8:26,27

   - First Corinthians 12:7; 14:1,2

   - Jude 20

3. The Bible tells us in Luke 6:37 that we should not judge others; however, there is a vast difference between having a critical and judgmental

attitude and evaluating the benefits or consequences of a particular situation. Read Romans chapter 14. What stands out to you in this chapter about evaluating our own individual conduct for the good of others around us? Are there any other scriptures or examples in the Bible that indicate evaluations had to be made and instructions given for the good of the people?

PRACTICAL APPLICATION

> But be ye doers of the word, and not hearers only,
> deceiving your own selves.
> — James 1:22

1. Have you ever stopped to consider who the individuals are that you are allowing to speak into your life? The authors of the books you read and the people you listen to on YouTube, television, and radio or those you follow on social media — who are they and what do they stand for? Take an inventory of who you're allowing to influence you. What is their character? Where were they educated? Who do they associate with and look up to? Are they believers who live a godly life both in public and in private? Based on this information, is there anyone you feel you need to disconnect from?

2. One way to hear God's voice more clearly is to sharpen your soul with the Word of God. This involves what the Bible calls *renewing your mind*. Take some time to reflect on Romans 12:1,2 and Ephesians 4:20-24 along with John 17:17, Ephesians 5:26, and Hebrews 4:12. In your own words, what steps would you need to take to renew your mind daily? What might the benefits of doing so look like?

3. As mentioned in the study questions above, a powerful way to hear God's voice more clearly is to pray in the language of the spirit, which the Bible calls *tongues*. Have you received the baptism of the Holy Spirit with the evidence of praying in other tongues? If so, are you praying in tongues regularly? If not, what is holding you back? If you have not received the baptism in the Holy Spirit but would like to, please call us at 1-800-742-5593. We would love to pray with you to receive this powerful gift from the Lord!

TOPIC

A Prophet's Submission to Authority

SCRIPTURES

1. **Hebrews 13:17** — Obey them that have the rule over you, and submit yourselves: for they watch for your souls, as they that must give account, that they may do it with joy, and not with grief: for that is unprofitable for you.

2. **1 Peter 5:6** — Humble yourselves therefore under the mighty hand of God, that he may exalt you in due time.

3. **Ephesians 4:11-13** — And he gave some, apostles; and some, prophets; and some, evangelists; and some, pastors and teachers; for the perfecting of the saints, for the work of the ministry, for the edifying of the body of Christ: till we all come in the unity of the faith, and of the knowledge of the Son of God, unto a perfect man, unto the measure of the stature of the fulness of Christ.

4. **Ephesians 2:20** — And are built upon the foundation of the apostles and prophets, Jesus Christ himself being the chief corner stone.

5. **1 Corinthians 9:2** — If I be not an apostle unto others, yet doubtless I am to you....

SYNOPSIS

The topic of submission to authority appears throughout the Bible. Christ embodied it as He surrendered His will to the will of the Father and laid His life down to redeem mankind. Although submission to authority is not a subject that many of us will rejoice over, it needs to be understood because it is often the one thing that will short-circuit our effectiveness as believers — both individually and corporately.

The emphasis of this lesson:

From the least to the greatest in the eyes of society, we are all commanded to submit to some form of authority in their lives. Even those in fivefold ministry, including prophets, are called to be in submission. This principle is designed to bring overall health and strength to the

Church. When God's people are submitted to one another, the Body of Christ is fully alive and functioning as it should.

Submission Is Part of Life

As the writer of Hebrews completed his letter to Jews who had converted to Christ, he gave them some important instructions. One of them deals with submitting to and giving honor to those who serve as leaders in the Church. He wrote:

> **Obey them that have the rule over you, and submit yourselves: for they watch for your souls, as they that must give account, that they may do it with joy, and not with grief: for that is unprofitable for you.**
>
> **— Hebrews 13:17**

This verse clearly states that we are to submit to the pastors and ministers God has placed over us, and that as we do, we make their job more enjoyable, which in turn benefits us.

If we really stop and think about it, everyone is to be in submission to authority in some area of their lives. First and foremost, as believers, we are called to live in submission to the lordship of Jesus. When we call Him "Lord," we are calling Him "*Boss.*" The Greek word for "Lord" most often used in the New Testament is *Kurios,* which means *Supreme Master* — there is no one higher. That means Jesus has absolute authority over our lives, and by calling Him "Lord," we have chosen to be bound by what He tells us to do in every area of our lives.

In the same way, in a marriage relationship, the wife is to be in submission to her husband, and in the family, the children in that household are to be in submission to their parents. Collectively, as citizens, we are to be in submission to governmental authorities, including those in law enforcement. Students are to be in submission to teachers and professors, and athletes are to be in submission to their coaches.

Submission is just a part of life that cannot be avoided. People who do not learn how to submit to authority eventually get into trouble, and some even end up in jail. That is why it is so vital for you to teach your children and grandchildren to submit to and honor authority. This will help place them on a good, solid path for their lives. Those who do not learn submission to authority grow up to be rebellious — unable to keep a job or get along well with others.

Even Ministry Leaders Are Called To Be in Submission to Authority

On the program, Rick shared how he is in submission to a group of men that he is accountable to, and they speak into his life regularly. They have a right to correct him if they sense something is not right and to ask him how he is doing in various areas of his life. Because he has made a choice to submit and open his life to these men, he remains very transparent with them.

Think about the apostle Paul who taught us in the Scriptures to be in submission to authority. He was traveling for months at a time to many different regions, yet he still had a group of people that he was accountable to — it was his team. The people he worked side by side with every day held Paul accountable and spoke into his life regularly. We can also see this in his letter to the Galatians, where he took Barnabas and Titus with him and humbly went before church leaders to share with them what he had been preaching to the Gentiles. He wanted to be sure they were in agreement, and Paul received their blessing when they recognized the call of God on his life (*see* Galatians 2:1-10).

In a similar way, Rick is accountable to the top members of his ministry team. Although he serves as a spiritual father to them in many ways, they have the right to speak into his life and address issues that need to be fixed. Just about every day, Rick will ask his team members questions like, "Have you read your Bible? Have you prayed in the spirit today?" At the same time, they might ask him the same questions, as well as whether he is exercising and taking care of himself. This level of accountability is healthy, needed, and appreciated all around.

Any minister of the Gospel — whether it's an apostle, prophet, pastor, teacher, or evangelist who doesn't have someone to be accountable to — is a minister who has no one watching over their soul. Without accountability, that minister will eventually get into trouble and won't know who to turn to when that happens.

Friend, you need people in your life that you can be accountable to. If you don't have someone, pray for God's guidance and look for individuals who are a little further along in life than you are — or those who are close to your age with the same heart for the Lord and seeking the same goals. It goes without saying that they should be people of godly character who you know care about your well-being and people you can really trust. Knowing that a person truly loves you and has your best interest at heart makes it much easier to be open with them and submit to them.

Everyone Needs Accountability Partners Who Can Speak Into Their Lives

As we saw in a previous lesson, the book of Jude describes people who no longer have accountability as *wandering stars*. Although they are shining the light of the Gospel through their ministry, they've swerved out of orbit from the people with whom God placed them. Without accountability, they will eventually get off track.

On the program, Rick said, "There are things I want to know about the people in ministry that I allow to speak into my life. For example, who are they orbiting life with? Are they in relationship with people that have a right to speak into their lives? Or are they just free-floaters?"

Free-floaters get into trouble because there's no one to bring them back into their God-assigned orbit. Regardless of how high up you go in ministry, you need someone to speak into your life — we all do. In fact, the more we can submit one to another, the more effective we will be in ministry.

The Bible says, "…God resisteth the proud, and giveth grace to the humble. Humble yourselves therefore under the mighty hand of God, that he may exalt you in due time" (1 Peter 5:5,6). As we humble ourselves by submitting to the authority of God in our lives and to those He has made us accountable to, He gives us grace to be more effective for His kingdom.

Please note that this principle of submission is not to make us into a domineering military troop that controls one another. Rather, it is for the overall health and strength of the life of the believer and the Church. Sadly, there are many in the Body of Christ who will only march to the beat of their own drum. They are so independently-minded that they have a hard time working together with anyone.

Think about what God could do through us as His Body if we would come together in unity! How many more things could we accomplish if we just worked together?

There Are 21 Spiritual Gifts Meant To Operate in the Church

What's interesting is that as you study the New Testament, you will see that there are three different places that talk about the unique gifts believers in the Body of Christ have been given. For example, in **Ephesians 4:11**, we find the fivefold ministry gifts Christ gave to the Church. These five gifts include apostles, prophets, evangelists, pastors, and teachers.

When we come to **First Corinthians 12:8-10**, we learn about the nine gifts of the Holy Spirit that are meant to operate within the Church for everyone's benefit. Here, Paul wrote, "For to one is given by the Spirit the word of wisdom; to another the word of knowledge by the same Spirit; to another faith by the same Spirit; to another the gifts of healing by the same Spirit; to another the working of miracles; to another prophecy; to another discerning of spirits; to another divers kinds of tongues; to another the interpretation of tongues."

Then in **Romans 12:6-8**, there are seven more gifts mentioned, which include prophecy, serving, teaching, exhorting or encouraging, giving, leadership, and mercy.

When we put all three of these groups of gifts together — the fivefold ministry gifts, the nine gifts of the Spirit, and the seven gifts mentioned in Romans 12 — we have a total of 21 spiritual gifts that are meant to operate in the Church. When all 21 gifts are in operation, it is a fulfillment of First John 4:17, which says, "…As he [Christ] is, so are we in this world."

For the Body of Christ to truly represent Christ in this world, each one of us need to be functioning in our God-given roles. For this to happen, we all need to find our tribe, stay with them, and be in submission to one another. This principle of submission, which Paul talks about in connection with all these gifts, has a great deal to do with us submitting to those within our tribe or jurisdiction. In other words, it means prophets should be submitted to other prophets, teachers to teachers, encouragers to encouragers, and so on. When we come together and are submitted one to another within our gift alignment that God has given us, divine order is established.

Now, each of the fivefold ministry gifts is responsible for a different district or region in the Body of Christ. It's amazing how God puts apostolic voices together and prophetic voices together, and the ultimate purpose of uniting members of the fivefold ministry offices is to build the Body. When each fivefold segment is effectively overseeing the area God has called them to, that is when the saints are effectively being edified and equipped and the Church is being built up in unity (*see* Ephesians 4:11-13). If fivefold ministers are not in submission to one another, it will likely diminish their overall effectiveness in edifying and equipping the saints.

True Submission to Authority Will Be Tested in Your Relationships

Realize that every relationship you are in will be tested. Jesus was in relationship with His disciples, and there came a point when His lordship was tested in each of their lives. Interestingly, all of them eventually passed the test — except Judas Iscariot.

A careful study of the Gospels reveals that all of Jesus' disciples called Him *Lord* — everyone except Judas. He was the one disciple who always called Jesus "Master," which in the original Greek text is the word for *teacher*.

Judas was a part of the team, but he was fabricating his allegiance to Jesus and the others. Although everyone else called Jesus "Lord" — which means *Supreme Master* — Judas was only willing to call Him "Teacher." He received Jesus as a teacher that he respected, but he never really submitted to Jesus' lordship.

A moment will always come in your relationships that reveals whether you're just along for the ride or you're genuinely in submission to authority, and it will be the moment of *disagreement*. Judas' major moment of disagreement came when Mary poured the exceedingly expensive perfume on Jesus' feet the night He was betrayed. Judas objected and said the perfume should have been sold and the money used for "the poor." Jesus rebuked Judas openly, and the rest is history (*see* John 12:3-8).

Like Judas, you can be in agreement with the authority over you, but that doesn't mean that you're in submission. A simple definition of submission is *submitting your mission in favor of another's.* When a moment of disagreement arises, it will reveal whether or not you're truly in submission.

We Must Remain in Submission
To the People and Place God Calls Us To

One of the most needed things that seems to be missing among many people who operate in the prophetic is submission to one another and submission to where God has placed them. Prophets cannot just pick and choose where they are going to operate. In the same way that pastors, evangelists, and teachers need to serve where God has placed them, prophets must also remain in their God-assigned region in order to be effective.

An example of this principle of submission is seen in the apostolic team of Paul and Barnabas as well as Paul and Silas. Again, Paul was in submission to his ministry team. No one knew him better than they did because they worked with him every day, and although they respected him as their leader, they had the right to speak into his life.

When we, as God's people, are in submission to one another and function in an orderly fashion, the Body of Christ lives. That is why it is so important — whether you are a churchgoer, a fivefold ministry leader, or anyone in between — that you know who your tribe is and know your jurisdiction, the area in which you are gifted.

God Has a Divine Assignment
With Your Name on It

As believers, all of us have a primary purpose, and that is to glorify God with our whole lives. Additionally, we each have a divine assignment — a specific vision and destiny that God created us to fulfill. As we live daily in relationship with Him and really press in to know Him, He begins to reveal the specific target He has designed us to hit.

Unfortunately, many Christians get a glimpse of their personalized calling, and they mistakenly believe that they are to immediately begin doing what God shows them. This is rarely the case. Instead, a process begins where God starts working on us to develop our character and prepare us for what He has for us to do.

Days, weeks, months, and even years pass, and many ups and downs are experienced. Slowly but surely, we move toward the well-defined destiny He has planned. In this preparation process, if we remain rightly aligned with our tribe, focused on and functioning in the place He has called us to, we will hit our target and be powerfully effective.

One of the worst things someone can do while waiting to carry out his or her calling is to begin moving around from one group to another. When someone is constantly changing from one ministry team to the next, it is often a sign that he is only being faithful to a group as long as everyone is in agreement with him. The moment people begin to disagree, this person bolts from the group, looking for others who will agree with him, and this creates spiritual instability in his life as a result.

Faithfully Serve Others As Though You Are Serving Jesus

When a person is truly in submission to authority, he or she remains with their leader. If a ministry seems to be a rotating door for employees or volunteers that come and go all the time, that's an indication there is something wrong. Either something is wrong in relationships, or something is wrong with authority.

The Bible says. "…Whatever you do, do it heartily, as to the Lord and not to men, knowing that from the Lord you will receive the reward of the inheritance; for you serve the Lord Christ" (Colossians 3:23,24 *NKJV*). We call Jesus "Lord" because He is our *Supreme Master* who is in command. Just as we wouldn't reject the Lord when He asks us to do something we don't like, we shouldn't retreat from those He has called us to serve.

If you think about it, being part of a mission with others helps you get to the vision God has called you to fulfill. That means being with the right people on the journey, in alignment with your tribe, and fulfilling God's purposes. This is true for apostles, prophets, evangelists, pastors, teachers, and everyone at every level in the Body of Christ.

When we are submitted to those in the orbit we have been placed in and to fellow believers in the Church, the Body of Christ can become the number one supernatural superpower in the world. United with one voice, we can speak and stop darkness in the name of Jesus! We can also see spiritual sons and daughters raised up to be clear-eyed, clear-minded warriors for the Lord.

How Will You Respond When Disagreement Takes Place?

Have you ever had an experience with someone in authority that revealed you weren't as submitted to them as you originally thought? Rick did, and it was an eye-opening experience indeed. Here's what he shared:

> When Denise and I were young in the ministry, I served under an amazing man of God, Dr. Bill Bennett. I loved Dr. Bennett, and initially, I was thrilled to call him my pastor. From my perspective, I was totally in submission to his authority, but when I started to notice things that made it a real challenge to work for him, my lack of submission was revealed.
>
> Honestly, some of his ways were just so rough and demanding, I really got bent out of shape with him. The situation became so unbearable to me that I ended up betraying him and leaving the church. For this reason, I understand what Judas Iscariot did because I acted in similar ways.
>
> As I said, throughout the time I served under Pastor Bennett, I felt like I was in submission to him. But that experience revealed my level of submission. I really failed the test in those early years of our ministry, and as a result, it threw me off course for several years. After floundering for a long time, I finally heard the convicting voice of the Holy Spirit and self-corrected my life to get back on track.
>
> Friend, you need to know that whether it's your boss, your pastor, your spouse, or your parents, a defining moment will always come to test whether or not you're really submitted to authority. You just can't avoid this issue if you are going to move forward in the Lord.
>
> I want to encourage you not to keep going around and around the same mountain of stubbornness and rebellion. Failing this test will cost you in every regard. It will cost you time, money, sleep, effectiveness, peace, and in so many other areas.

If you have a problem submitting to the person in authority over you, don't just quit and say, "I'm done with you." Instead, pray and ask God for help. He will show you a way to work things out respectfully, without bypassing or evading authority, which He never does.

It's better to be corrected by someone in authority who is imperfect than to rebel against that person's leadership, even if you think you're right. Remember, God sees everything accurately, and He is keeping perfect records of all that has happened. As we saw in First Peter 5:6 earlier, if you humble yourself in submission under the mighty hand of God, He will exalt you in due time!

STUDY QUESTIONS

> **Study to shew thyself approved unto God, a workman that needeth not to be ashamed, rightly dividing the word of truth.**
> **— 2 Timothy 2:15**

1. Regardless of how far you advance in ministry, you need people speaking into your life whom you are accountable to. Who in your life has that right and asks questions about how you are living? According to Ecclesiastes 4:9-12; Proverbs 27:17; and Malachi 3:16, what can you look forward to receiving from the relationships you have with people in your tribe and jurisdiction?

2. Judas never called Jesus "Lord" because he never submitted to His lordship. He only received Jesus as a respected teacher. How about you? Is Jesus the "Lord" — Supreme Master — of your life, or is He just a good Teacher, Prophet, and Savior? What evidence might Jesus point to that displays He is truly Lord of your life?

3. As a believer, your primary purpose is to glorify God with your whole life. Additionally, you have a divine assignment — a specific vision and destiny that He created for you to fulfill. In what ways has God uniquely gifted you? What do you most enjoy doing for God and for others? Do you know the special assignment God has for you? If not, begin to seek His face and ask Him to reveal His calling on your life.

PRACTICAL APPLICATION

But be ye doers of the word, and not hearers only,
deceiving your own selves.
—James 1:22

The Bible says, "Obey your spiritual leaders, and do what they say. Their work is to watch over your souls, and they are accountable to God. Give them reason to do this with joy and not with sorrow. That would certainly not be for your benefit" (Hebrews 13:17 *NLT*).

1. In all honesty, what is your current attitude toward your spiritual leaders?

2. Are you doing what they ask, or are you regularly dismissing and ignoring their wishes?

3. Think for a moment if you were in their position and you were leading someone like you. Do you think your actions and attitude make their job a joy or a burden?

4. If you were leading you, what changes would you ask "you" to make?

Knowing that we are to do everything we do "as unto the Lord," walk back through these same four questions and apply them to your relationships in other areas of authority in your life, such as at work or home.

NOTES

Joseph Z. *Demystifying the Prophetic — Understanding the Voice of God for the Coming Days of Fire*. Shippensburg, PA: Harrison House Publishers, 2024.

A Prayer To Receive Salvation

If you've never received Jesus as your Savior and Lord, now is the time for you to experience the new life Jesus wants to give you! To receive God's gift of salvation that can be obtained through Jesus alone, pray this prayer from your heart:

Jesus, I repent of my sin and receive You as my Savior and Lord. Wash away my sin with Your precious blood and make me completely new. I thank You that my sin is removed, and Satan no longer has any right to lay claim on me. Through Your empowering grace, I faithfully promise that I will serve You as my Lord for the rest of my life.

If you just prayed this prayer of salvation, you are born again! You are a brand-new creation in Christ! Would you please let us know of your decision by going to **renner.org/salvation**? We would love to connect with you and pray for you as you begin your new life in Christ.

Scriptures for further study: John 3:16; John 14:6; Acts 4:12; Ephesians 1:7; Hebrews 10:19,20; 1 Peter 1:18,19; Romans 10:9,10; Colossians 1:13; 2 Corinthians 5:17; Romans 6:4; 1 Peter 1:3

Notes

Notes

CLAIM YOUR FREE RESOURCE!

As a way of introducing you further to the teaching ministry of Rick Renner, we would like to send you FREE of charge his teaching, "How To Receive a Miraculous Touch From God" on CD or as an MP3 download.

How To Receive a Miraculous Touch From God
Rick Renner

CD36

R RENNER

In His earthly ministry, Jesus commonly healed *all* who were sick of *all* their diseases. In this profound message, learn about the manifold dimensions of Christ's wisdom, goodness, power, and love toward all humanity who came to Him in faith with their needs.

☑ **YES, I want to receive Rick Renner's monthly teaching letter!**

Simply scan the QR code to claim this resource or go to:
renner.org/claim-your-free-offer

Connect

W I T H   U S !

R renner.org

f facebook.com/rickrenner • facebook.com/rennerdenise

▶ youtube.com/rennerministries • youtube.com/deniserenner

⊙ instagram.com/rickrrenner • instagram.com/rennerministries_
instagram.com/rennerdenise

www.ingramcontent.com/pod-product-compliance
Lightning Source LLC
Chambersburg PA
CBHW071642040426
42452CB00009B/1732